Paper Crowns
and the Glass House

By
Eliza Sinead

AOS Publishing, 2024

Copyright © 2024

Eliza Sinead

ISBN: 978-1-990496-95-0

Cover Design: Chanelle Poupart

Visit AOS Publishing's website:
www.aospublishing.com

Part One
The Drowning

My face falls with the grace of snow
As you walk in the room,
My marionette wakens.
The droplets pooling
On my forehead
Have nowhere left to run

I see your face in the morning frost
Myself in each crystalized petal
The steam rising from my chamomile tea is
The only reminder I'm still alive

    – *still not clean*

the scent of the candle allures me,
but it's the numbing ache
after the touch of the flickering flame
that makes me feel at home

You—
You were supposed to protect me.
Hide me from the dangers of the world, not inflict them on me.
You were supposed to be defensive of my heart,
Not be the one to break it before any lover got the chance.

your fist collides
with my freshly-bruised skin

but your words hurt the most

"just a worthless, stupid bitch"

I feel like kicking and screaming and crying and punching and throwing up and screaming and pulling out my hair and crying and scratching at my skin and kicking and screaming and screaming and screaming until I physically cannot any longer. I feel like thrashing my arms about like a toddler and tearing apart photographs and cutting tiny pieces out of my sheets and punching a hole through the wall and ripping the fairy lights off my bed and tearing the clothes off my body and smashing the window because I cannot breathe in this tiny room.

But I do not speak or move.

She was a supernumerary rainbow until he stomped over her with his mud-smothered boots.

You have taught me to live with pain like no other.
Tell me, will it hurt more if I stay or if I go?

i cleanse my skin with pointed brushes
paint leaks from my legs,
dripping on the bathroom tiles
which are cool against my cheeks
music up, the shower running
so no one can hear my screams,
i cry until i am paralysed
by the poltergeist embodying me

I swear
To Lucifer,
If you mess
With me,
I will pull
The knife
From my back
Still warm
With my blood
And carve
My name
Across your face

    - I am the Devil's child

And like a child who has just been yelled at by their mother, I go back to the person who hurt me for comfort.

Every night when she was left alone
And the house had fallen silent,
She would weep until her eyes burned
And her lungs filled with water
But when morning came, and the roosters crowed
Marking the start of the day
She would put on her mask and walk out the door
As if everything were truly okay

Cold eyes glaring
Smile crooked and daring
I ran for the back door
But he was too fast

I hid myself in the laundry
But not before his arm caught me
And the words flew
Out of his mouth:

"I'm gonna kill you"
He floored me
Turned me around
And pounded his fist into my back

I feel like I am walking on a tightrope made of ice.

It is so loud
In this quiet room—
So many voices,
Yet no lips move

We lay on your bed
My head on your chest
On top of your covers
Your door slightly open
I gaze up at your eyes
Feeling safe in your arms

I hate that part of me
Still thinks it was love

We lay on your bed
My head on your chest
On top of your covers
Your door slightly open,
Your fingers trace my arms
Before wondering to my torso,
To my pant line,
Underneath.

They are lost.
I try to help them find their way back to you
But they are stubborn and refuse to listen.

It takes link by link from the metal chain
That is tightening around my heart

Force-feeds me pebbles

Pokes holes in my lungs

- Depression

I poured myself into you
Then you left and I was empty

There are so many scattered pieces of my heart
Too lost to find their way back to each other
Forever damned to float through my body
Alone.

My mind is a cave
Infested with bats
And all the exits
Are sealed by rocks.

Each time he touched me,
I'd feel my body tremble
Warm tears streamed down my face
I'd look around my room
But only see your orange walls

Venomous words
Plunge from my mouth,
Taking the form of daggers,
They fire into the hearts
Of those I love

I don't like the dark side of me

When I wake up
Still half asleep,
I turn around to hold you
Then the weight of your absence—
The weight of what you did—
Comes crashing down
Like a ton of bricks
Falling
From the top of the Empire State Building,
Leaving my body Bruised.
Bloody.
Broken.

You played the ghostwritten character so well
I fell in love with someone who never existed.

You say
I would have left
if you told me,
I tell you that is the point

　　How dare you take away my choice in the name of love

My emotions are so wild
I feel like clawing my brain out
With my fingernails

The lines of love become blurry
When you grow up always associating it with pain.

You're creating generations of
Broken homes and lost souls
By staying when
You know you should go
Let go of your excuse
And lead by example
The concept of staying for the kids
Needs to be dismantled

Children learn all they know from you

I'm tired of protecting our
House of Glass.
If you didn't want it broken,
You shouldn't have thrown so many stones

Is it too much to ask
For love to just be
All
That you promised me?

For the first time in a long time, I was scared of the person in front of me. As you were screaming in my face, a twisted part of my brain was waiting, hoping, preparing for your fist on my cheek. Something to make me feel alive. Something to give me reason to leave. As if the spit from your tongue dripping off my lashes wasn't reason enough.

I want to cry until I'm drowning in tears
This life is so hard, why can't I end it?
I just need love, but that's too much to ask
Is there anyone out there who will understand?

This life is so hard, why can't I end it?
I know it's not right, I'll be better by morning
Is there anyone out there who will understand?
I'm not alone, the voices are angels

I know it's not right, I'll be better by morning
It's all in my mind, or that's what they tell me
I'm not alone, the voices are angels
Sent up from Hell to personally guide me

It's all in my mind, or that's what they tell me
The visions are lies, that's not a dead body
Sent up from Hell to personally guide me
Swallow these pills so you're not psychotic

The visions are lies, that's not a dead body
Oh how I wish somebody had warned me
Swallow these pills so you're not psychotic
They think I'm insane but I'm not a danger– mostly.

Oh how I wish somebody had warned me
I just need love but that's too much to ask
They think I'm insane but I'm not a danger. Mostly,
I want to cry until I'm drowning in tears.

There is nothing like a crazy woman
Whom you fail to admit you turned mad.

Always the illusion
        Never the art
Always the poet
        Never the love

As the first-born lamb to the black sheep,
I never stood a chance

  Neither did he

They put me under the knife and pulled me from beneath the blade in the same breath

Tell me what I'm supposed to do with that

What is love if not violent?
What is love if not pain?
What is love if not betrayal?
What is love if not a game?
What is love if not lies?
What is love if not self-deprecation?
What is love if not fear?
What is love if not invalidation?

If this is not love, then I don't know its name
For all of my time, love has been everything but safe.

Part Two
Resurrection

It's time to dust the cobwebs in your mind
The spiders have nested there long enough.

You've painted a picture
Of who you think I am in your head

But you don't know my colours

They say that I'm mature for my age like it's a compliment
Little do they know I never had a say

My frozen heart has defrosted,
But it is not yet warm enough
For an all-encompassing love

All my life I have wanted children
But now that I've grown
That feeling is gone
As I realise I've been a parent all along

It has been two years since I moved
Two years since the lightbulb blew
Yet still it sits unchanged in my family's bathroom
I have stopped reminding them it is out

Both a metaphor and a fact

I am slowly replacing
my daggered gown
with paper crowns
as I learn
how to clean
our spilled blood

Breaking the cycle

I wonder if she knows I can see the tears she never cried
I wonder if she knows I can see how hard she always tried
I wonder if she knows it's okay that she didn't always get it right
I hope she knows she has strengths in many other places

I wonder if she knows I know I broke her heart
I wonder if she knows she equally tore me apart
I hope she knows I still love her endlessly

I wonder if she knows I know how much she gave up
I wonder if she knows how truly grateful we are
I wonder if she knows she makes me proud

I wonder if she knows I wish she'd noticed the signs
I wonder if she knows I just needed help at the time
I hope she knows I never meant to hurt her

I wonder if she knows I still sometimes break down at night
I wonder if she knows now how to be there next time
I wonder if she knows I'm worried she never will

I wonder if she knows I know it's not easy
I wonder if she knows I know she feels guilty
I wonder if she knows I just want her to see me

I wonder if she knows in the end this won't matter
I wonder if she knows she's still an inspiration
I hope she knows my love for her will always outweigh the pain

How do you write about family
When they are one of your worst triggers
And your greatest love?
I would do anything to protect them,
And yet I couldn't stay

You can't grow
In the same soil
That prevented you
From flowering in the first place

I would look in the mirror
And I'd tell myself
You are fat
You are ugly
You are nothing
I'd look myself in the eyes and
Watch as I cried,
Believing I deserved nothing better—
That everyone would be happier if I were gone.

I was wrong.

my bones grind as I howl at the moon,
grazed knees mixing with dirt.
if only I were as beautiful as stars,
nevertheless I emulate their spirit.
burning.   burning.   burning.
only to fall with chaotic grace,
they cannot cease my fire.
even through death my words will live on

The funniest thing about "nice" guys
Is that they believe they're being wronged
When suddenly they don't
Hold all the power

we don't owe you shit

My favourite 'struggle' to hear men complain about is how hard it is to be a straight white male in this day and age. Of course, you'll notice when more competition is accepted into the race. You're simply admitting there is a problem.

You're right.
It's not *all* men.
But it is enough men
For it to be a serious Problem.
We are done absorbing your misogyny
Silently.

If you're the man shouting
"It's not all men!"
Then you have misunderstood.
And it is probably you.

You are part of the Problem.

I'm not a doll
You can't pull me back by a string
Every time you get bored
Or horny

go ahead
tie me to the stake,
the licking flame
excites my heels.
scream as it
engulfs my body
but fails to penetrate
my skin
      (gather round as I whisper)
"if I were you
I would *run*"

"Tie me to the stake," I bait
I'll wear the title with pride
"Thy witch," they call
Thy witch I am
If independence
Integrity
Intelligence
Are indeed a crime
Punishable by death

Women are magic
They are so much more than the credit they receive
Especially in this world of hegemony

just stand there.
Broken and Mauling
daydreaming
of all that could be
in an infinite sky
of milky way lines
the stars dance in Your eyes
can you not see them
in the mirror child?
Your mind is your only limit

shooting stars

It's a candle flickering in the darkness, refusing to burn out

hope

I will rise from the ashes,
Not as a phoenix, but from the grave
I have died many times
But am still alive to this day

She grew tired of waiting
So she tied up her hair
Tore off her corset
And she rescued herself
Before anyone else could take the credit

I no longer care about the image they paint
I am okay with being their villain
If it means I am free from their chains

Dear reader,
In the darkest hour
In the dead of night
When the demons puppet your mind
Know there is a new day blooming
And it will shine just for you

What is love if not pulling yourself out of the pit while the world continues, oblivious?

Part Three
Amor

I've spent years
Breaking down
The cage
That has held
Me captive

Now that it's open
I don't know how to fly
So I hover
At the entry
Praying
One day I will
Soar

    – Have faith in your wings

Sometimes we need to break a little so we can learn to see the light through the cracks

when I look at my dog
smiling up at me,
tongue hanging from
the side of her mouth,
eyes full
of pure joy and love
as she gives me
her paw to hold,
I know everything will be okay

Staring at blank pages
Sitting bare skin in a damp bed
Missing you
Waiting for these pages to write themselves
Reminiscing our love
I can almost feel your lips trace my neck,
A soft melody against my yearning skin

You counted your flaws like I counted calories
Even in your darkest moments, I always saw your light

A wilted flower can still bloom
If you take time to tend to its roots

When the pain is all-encompassing
And I can't get out of bed
I look for small miracles
And make a list inside my head

Christmas decorations   candles

butterflies   cups of tea   flowers

pets

the scent of a new book

poetry   paintings

colours

rain rolling in over mountains

waterfalls   pot plants

hot chocolate

a baby's first laugh   fairy lights

There is beauty all around
Sometimes we just forget to look

Don't settle for less
Than all you want for your best friend

You deserve greatness, too

On your gravestone
They are not going to write about your
Stretch marks,
Cellulite,
Or scars
They are going to write about how special you were
How loved you still are

A secret I wish I could tell younger me
Is that she has always been enough

    – *You are, too*

The unconditional love of a pet
Can make all the difference

Animals have the gentlest souls
Their devotion we may never deserve

Dear younger me,
We made it.

And I have never been prouder.
I promise to keep chasing our dreams for you.

I long for a love
where the only surprises
are picnic dates,
love letters,
and flowers

I would tear the sea
Apart for you
For I know
How you so
Fear its depth

Will you rest your head on my chest,
My hand in your hair,
While we lay
Underneath
A willow tree?

We can point at
The clouds
Through the sun-speckled space
Amid the leaves,
Reciting poetry

I am having the time of my life unravelling
the story board that is you

I let my soul slip out of my body,
Momentarily free from the heavy grasp of the world.
I run my fingers through your burgundy hair
I trace your jawline
My skin so pale against your warmth,
I gently find my lips against yours
Before I retreat from the stares
That were never really there.
I go back to my notebook
To write you again,
Aching for your love,
Terrified of the possibility.

The one who made me realise

Slow dancing
Under kitchen lights
Cheap nail polish
Flaking on the tiles
The constellations in your eyes
I could fall in forever—
Let me know, darling,
If you will be there when I land

There are no words warm enough
To describe the feeling of being loved

Know that all this time
I have heard you calling,
I have been following
The melody of your voice
To find my way back to you—
To find my way home

I am sorry for all you have been through. All the pain that has been caused by those who were supposed to love you. All the scars you hide. All the walls you have built because you don't know how else to stay safe. All the weight you carry on your shoulders. All the times you have been betrayed. I am sorry. From one stranger to another, you are enough. You have always been and forever will be enough. I am sorry if you have not been shown that.

You matter, please stay

What if you spent all that time and energy on loving yourself instead of tearing yourself down?

How magical would that be?

She looked up at the stars
Hoping to one day be
As beautiful as them,
Not realising that she already was

In the end I'm no longer surprised that I made it.
Though the mountains were high
And their edges grew more jaded,
I have always had myself.

I feel it
In my fingertips
Every time they pick up
A pen
Every time they
Dance
Over my keyboard

They are made of magic
Full of life
Full of worlds
That you may never understand

I am a Poet

There is room enough for all our crowns
Your time will come to wear the gowns

Treat your body with kindness
It is your forever home

You taste like poetry
I can never get enough

The way she turns her pain into art has always astounded me

Darling, you are magic

The spark of a match
In the dead of night
Always reminds me of you

Why cut your wings when you were born to fly?

If your to-do list includes

> Getting out of bed
> Drinking water
> Brushing your teeth
> Having something to eat
> Showering

And one thing is all you manage to accomplish, I am proud of you.

Recovery is hard, consistency is key

Happiness is snuggling with your pets and reading a new book. It's planting cottage flowers and making coffee from a pot. It's meeting new people and it's staying inside. It's writing your feelings and feeling the sunshine. It's baking and painting and dancing and singing. It's music, it's poems, it's butterflies, it's knitting. There are so many things that make life worth living. You will find your way.

The doubt of the crowd
Transforms to all but a whisper
When you start to believe
In yourself

In the end she was grateful for her thorns,
Without them she wouldn't truly be a rose

What is love if not patient?
What is love if not kind?
What is love if not loyal?
What is love if not compromise?
What is love if not gentle?
What is love if not sweet?
What is love if not forgiveness?
What is love if not feeling complete?

If you don't recognise this love, create it my dear
Be your own love story, you have nothing to fear